MEMORIZING SHADOWS

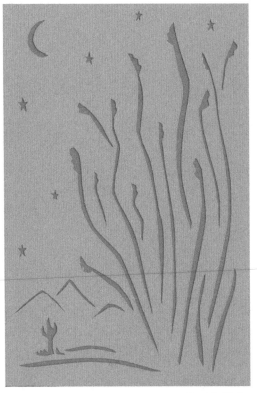

Ocotillo Nights

MEMORIZING SHADOWS

Inspiration from the Arizona Trail

poems and images by

Heidi Elizabeth Blankenship

Shanti Arts Publishing
Brunswick, Maine

MEMORIZING SHADOWS
Inspiration from the Arizona Trail

Published by Shanti Arts Publishing
Designed by Shanti Arts Designs

Shanti Arts LLC
193 Hillside Road
Brunswick, Maine 04011
shantiarts.com

Printed in the United States of America

ISBN: 978-1-941830-32-1 (softcover)
ISBN: 978-1-941830-30-7 (digital)

Library of Congress Control Number: 2017934497

For all my ancestors,
my mother and grandmothers,
and for the earth,
without whom life would not be possible.

Ribbon Falls

CONTENTS

PREFACE

These poems originated on the Arizona Trail as I walked from Mexico to Utah during the spring of 2012. Many were scribbled between footsteps, some while paused at scenic vistas, others at dusk before sleep descended.

The artwork was fashioned after photographs taken while hiking. Germans call the art form *scherenschnitte,* and the Chinese call it *Jianzhi,* but I just call them paper cuts (similar to wood cuts) because that's what I get from making them. Originals measure 4" by 6" and were made with cardstock.

The Arizona Trail was my first long thru-hike, and I didn't really know what to expect. From Mexico to Patagonia, I had the company of my trail mentors, Barb Zinn and Li Brannfors, and from Patagonia north to Utah, I hiked solo. I was never alone, however, as so many people helped me along the way, and many others walked with me in spirit. The trail itself became my guide and every sunrise encouraged me to walk. These are the words that joined me from the ether and I am happy to share them with you. Enjoy!

ACKNOWLEDGMENTS

My journey and the production of this book would never have been possible without help from many people. I am so grateful for everyone who has helped me along this path. I especially want to thank Barb Zinn and Li Brannfors, my incredible long-distance hiking inspirations, for all their help as mentors. Thanks to Barb for coaching me in water caches, talking me through the trail, and showing me southern Arizona. Thanks to Li for technical support, maps, and helpful hints.

I am deeply indebted to Hilda Smith for allowing my world to explode all over hers, continually, in the form of food cache packing and map marking, and in the creation of the paper cuts. Hilda deserves a medal for putting up with me! Without the editorial assistance and encouragement from Barbara Romney Galler, Margaret Pettis, Wendy Blankenship, and Thea Gavin, this poetry would only exist on crumpled pocket pages. Special thanks to Christine Cote at Shanti Arts Publishing, for incredible patience and enthusiasm while bringing this work to the world.

Thanks to Dan Alberts for starting the trip off by giving me the first ride; Bonnie Hamlin and Lupe for shelter and encouragement before the hike in Sonoita; Meg Gilbert for shelter and a knee brace in Patagonia; Brian, Susan, and Tia Bellew for adopting me during the big snowstorm in Tucson and for being such amazing humans to a complete stranger; Maria and Lloyd Wilson for ice water and a sweet prayer near the Gila River; Zac O'Neal for bringing cold lemonade to me on the trail in the Mazatzals (!); Jessica Pope for shelter and support in Flagstaff; Jean Rukkila for poetry, great conversation, and dinner in Flagstaff; Tony and Kelly Miller for encouragement and going out of their way to help with a North Rim water cache; Steve Bridgehouse for support on both rims and nagging me to publish in full color; Jeau Allen for a ride and a delicious prickly pear popsicle at my second ending; Mark Wunner and staff at the Backcountry Information Center at Grand Canyon National Park for a permit and flexibility with my work schedule; and staff at Saguaro National Park for providing a permit. I appreciate Dr. Todd Mangum, Dr. Eric Toder, Roger Patterson, and Felix Tatarovich for their skills in the art of keeping my bones, muscles, and organs happy on this hike and all others. Thanks to Sue Morgan and Mike Salamacha for retrieving me with open hearts and big smiles despite the impending storm, and to Mike for storing my truck for the duration, for snagging that historic ledger (!), and for so much encouragement.

Thanks to all the people who preserve the vision, work with the land, and keep the AZT alive. Many thanks to Matthew J. Nelson for support and enthusiasm. And thanks to the trail itself.

Much love and support came from my family, and I am grateful to all of them for rooting me on even though the idea may have sounded a little crazy by their standards. Thanks to Wendy and Dad for providing me with fruit and garden veggies for my dehydrated trail foods. Thanks to my parents for teaching me persistence and encouraging me to pursue my dreams. Thanks to Dad for teaching me how to draw.

There are millions more to thank — human and non-human, seen and unseen.

I am so blessed for the part you've all played in every volume of my life. Thank you!

Heidi Elizabeth Blankenship

Huachuca Foothills

FIRST STRETCH

Best to have it all the first day:
trail too steep,
pack too heavy,
a body too soft from winter,
snowbanks
encrusted with ice,
torrents of wind
screeching
over the crest of the Huachucas
like raging phantoms
in an unexpectedly cold night
tinged, strangely,
with cigarette smoke.
Best to have it all right away,
so you know
precisely
what to expect.

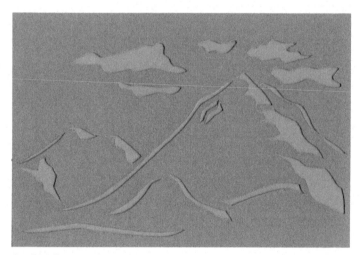

Canelo Hills

CELEBRATE

Every day
    there is something
        to fall in love with:
            bright orange poppies
            bobbing their heads
            beside the trail,
            the long arms of ocotillos
            leaved to their tips
            and ready to burst into scarlet plumes,
            the tangled bodies of saguaros
            leaning slowly into one another
            in a silent dance
            that lasts a lifetime.
All around,
    the world
        is full
            of celebration.

Santa Rita Mountains

BEYOND PISTOL HILL

Time
is measured
between the shade
of saguaros.

BAREFOOT

Mystical
clear
water
luxury
swirls around toes
and ankles,
tiny pebbles
and sand
stirred
by current
massage
feet.
Los Cienegas Creek,
a ribbon of pleasure
beneath the first saguaro
tilting on the hill.
Tall trees
arc overhead,
every rough edge
trimmed in green.
There is nothing
anywhere
in hundreds of miles
more
divine
than
this.

Alligator Bark

SHADE

In case you need some,
in miles and miles
of Sonoran desert,
the only real shade
is beneath the highway
in long tunnels
filled with noise
and dark questions,
ripe with rattlesnakes
and the fresh tracks
of mountain lions,
and every other
imaginary creature
that just might grab
your feet.

White Canyon Wilderness

THE RAINBOW

Walking with the sun
through an explosion of flowers:
lily, blue dick, purple parsley,
        evening primrose, yellow mariposa,
skunkbush, globemallow, daisy,
        aster, eriogonum, shocking pink
penstemon, mentzelia, mesquite,
        fairy duster, giant heliotrope, bright
orange poppies, tiny golden drops,
        pink phlox, purple verbena,
mountain bluebells, cliffrose,
        redbud, fendler bush, prickly pear,
ocotillo, lupine,
like a rainbow of precious jewels
spread across the land.
What a gift,
these days and days
just to love them,
just to love.

Lovely One

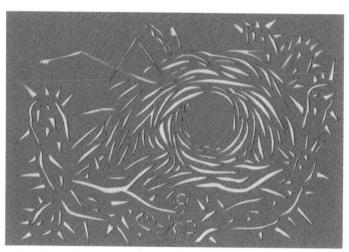

Cholla Nest

GIVE IN

What miles?
What time?
Be tempted!
Be seduced!
Dip your feet!
Linger
in the shade
of tall oaks
and sycamores.
Live
here
this moment

WARNINGS

All the way
they warned me:
Bark Scorpions!
Smugglers!
Lions!
But what of the mad dogs
in Enzenberg Canyon
hidden from view,
bellowing from rocky ridges
with ungodly yelps and yowls;
or the bees
in the Black Hills
and at Pusch Ridge,
darkening the sky
in a gigantic
buzzing swarm,
part hover, part motion?
A gun won't save you —
not here —
but if you whisper
and
tip-toe,
walk faster than light,
be still in your mind
and bend with the shadows,
you might escape
just once
without notice.

Four Peaks Wilderness

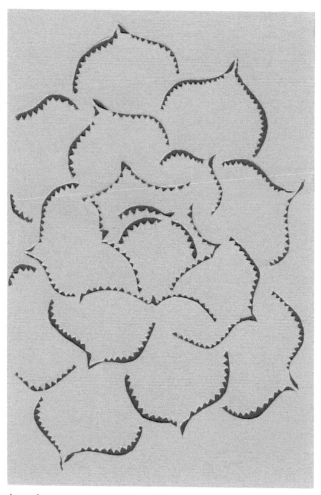

Agave Lace

COW PIES

Top of the list
of the things I won't miss
includes
the horrific
dizzying thrum
of a hundred
thousand
black flies
rising
off cow pies,
hovering like
an enormous
alien ship
with pulsating walls,
disrupting the silence,
startling my steps
in the wildest places
of Arizona.

BEE OPERAS

Songs stick and fade
during long hours of walking
and sometimes
in a lonely moment
I create operas
(don't tell!),
belting out
nonsensical songs
in every possible
musical genre
to everything
and everyone
in listening range;
songs
that
fortunately for you
will never be heard again
except
perhaps
by cacti,
a million bees,
and
meadow larks.

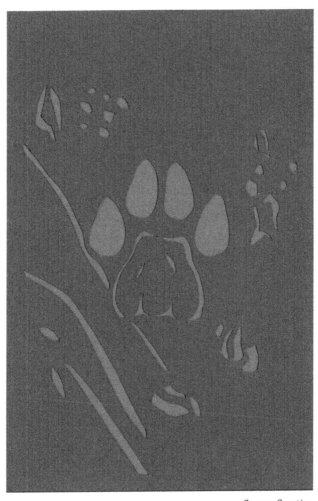

Cougar Greeting

FULL

Keep your life,
wherever you may be,
and I'll keep mine,
every day
wandering back
into myself,
each step
a little closer,
carrying my heart
across the desert,
returning
again and again
to the earth
below me,
windblown,
consumed
by billions
of stars.

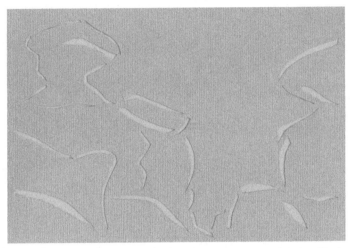

Wilderness of Rocks

Dancing Yucca

SUPERIOR, AZ

I order a second plate of enchiladas,
    having already devoured the first.
Hands on her hips she asks,
    "Honey, where you gonna put that?"
It's hard to explain,
    having already downed
that second plate
    for two weeks
dream walking
    on the trail.

IN PINE

"Don't you get scared out there?"
She asked, bending in close, half-whispering.
"I'd be afraid something would get me," she said.

What is this fear of the wild?
I would much rather be jumped by a mountain lion
than kidnapped by a serial killer
or mutilated in a car accident.

Death happens.
Everywhere.
Anywhere.
Everyday.

One thing is certain —
whatever has you grinding
your teeth at night
or clenching your jaw and screaming,
will find you
on the long trail,
be it daylight or dark,
and it will rip your heart out anew
with demons
and revelations
that plant you on the ground
in awe of their depth.
Your own mind
is the biggest challenge
out there.

On Trail

Gila Mentor

BAD DAY

Awakened
hot and grumpy
my map suddenly transformed into Sanskrit verse
    and I walk too far
        in the wrong direction
for water
because I can't. Decipher. Sanskrit.
And if there was a decent road in this
God-forsaken country,
    God knows I'd hitch out.
My pack is too heavy,
        my knees hurt,
          the vultures don't want me.
I stop for an early lunch in the only speck of shade,
ants crawling all over me.

A bee ambles over and afraid of a sting,
I tell him to leave
and he turns,
clambers over tiny pebbles,
stops a pace away,
and dies.
    Miserable wreck of a human.
I pack things up,
    stumble onward,
    still grumbling.
Then   A LOUD HISS stops me.
      Heart pounds.
      Breath quickens.
Every sense searching,
scanning the margins between cactus and shrubs
for the origin of sound —
        and there
        blocking the trail from edge to edge,
        bright orange, striped black
        sun-faded, beady, scaled skin,
        tongue whipped out,
        dark bottomless eyes watching,

the LARGEST LIZARD
       in the United States,
one of the only
VENOMOUS lizards in the whole world,
ready to dart or bite or do whatever
Heloderma suspectum will do.
I stare.
Gila Monster stares back.
We wait.
One minute. Two minutes. Five minutes.
Ten.
Neither of us move.
Finally
Gila Monster turns, faces away.
I exhale, inching slowly around the reptile,
dodging cactus spines and pricklies,
alert
once again
alive
and ready
to walk.

WHY

We all need
to revive our spirits
somehow,
remind ourselves
we are still alive,
discover air so sweet
it induces euphoria
in our souls;
to experience all life,
remembering
each precious second
deep down
in our marrow.

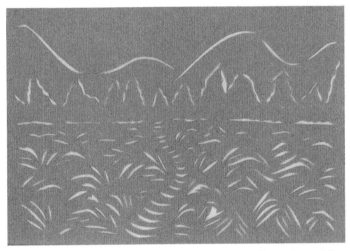

Grassy Superstitions

Perfect Balance

BACKPACK

Each morning
my companion
squeaks
from
a different angle,
be it a strap
or a buckle,
shoulder or waist,
from some kind
of unseen friction,
always
loud,
always
unstoppable,
splitting
the quiet
in time
with my
footsteps.

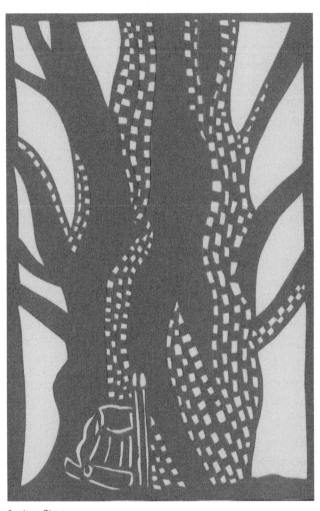

Juniper Giant

SUPERSTITION WILDERNESS

The mother of all
    alligator juniper trees
        lives beside the trail.

Weathered and smooth
    with a thick swath of bark
        twisting
    over her massive trunk
        and around her limbs,
    she is charred by fires
        but still thriving.

Oh, to spend the rest of my days
    exploring those magical limbs,
        to feel her wisdom
            pulsing through cambium.

PROVISIONS

At the end of the day:
backpack
pocket knife
stove
sleeping pad
shoes.

After all these miles:
Peanut M&M's
Tinkyada gluten-free pasta
cheese
chocolate
carrots.

At the end of the trail,
what do we really need?
Beating heart
clean air
pure water
shelter
rest.

Mesquite Sleep

COTTONWOOD WASH

Rocky and dry,
I expected no more than a puddle
for a spring
in this wash,
but then a jungle appeared
around a bend;
tangles of vines dangling
from sycamore and cottonwood,
flowing water
bordered suddenly
in unexpected green.
The best sleeping spot
is at day's end,
legs too tired to move.
Out of the wind,
low in the canyon,
beneath mesquite,
I snuggle into lush grass,
watch the light fade on hillsides
dotted with saguaro and prickly pear,
sip the same water
that tiny bird neighbors drink,
and listen to the poorwills
calling all around.

In the Clouds

East Verde

BLOCKADE

Big Black Bull
    won't budge.
Sawed Horns.
    Big Balls.

My trail.
    His trail.
Deadlock.

Crazy human:
    I sing
    The Beatles,
    The Monkeys,
    Nine Inch Nails,
    shaking hiking poles
    skyward.

He moves.
    Finally.
        Just enough.

DRINK

Alder Creek,
Roger's Creek,
Reavis Spring.
Drinking these waters
I am part
of this great wide universe.
Sycamore Creek,
bathing tiny fish and spotted boatmen.
Oak Spring,
gushing at the base
of a massive tree.
Polk Spring,
feeding a bright path of watercress.
McFarland Canyon,
waters flowing beneath
majestic Douglas Fir.
From the mouth of the earth,
from the skin and the folds
of the earth,
to my mouth
and into my veins.

I am part of the sky,
the earth,
the waters,
and you too,
drinking from your source —
we are all intrinsically one,
connected by our cells
through water
to this great, wide universe.

Clear Creek

Naked Stone

MAZATZAL FIRE

Rocks like fallen sunset
gleam
between
scorched trees.
Blackened earth
slowly reclaims
with tiny green sprouts.
Wilderness sings
despite the devastation,
filling the atmosphere
with a deep,
penetrating
buzz
of silence.
We must love the earth
with every step,
even paths through ashes,
snagged and bloodied
by thorns and catclaw.
Even here,
through the burn.

SKELETONS

Screaming Trees
was just the name of a band
until I walked
through black forest,
devastated by wildfire.
I thought it was howling coyotes,
a pack
following close,
tracing my steps,
and I quickened my pace.
Then suddenly
I realized
it was the trees
with the wind
rushing past
their charred,
barren
trunks,
thousands of skeleton
sticks
screaming.

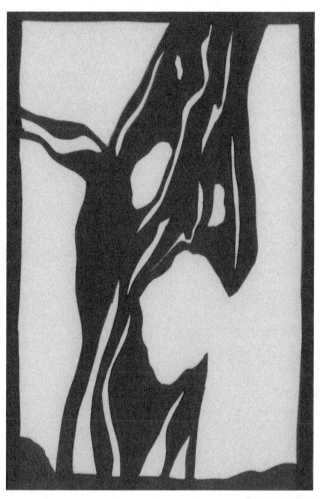

Screaming Tree

AFTER LAKE MARY

You have to know
what you're doing.
Start
with your feet.
Feel
everything
all the way up
into your heart
as your body moves
from mountains
to grasslands,
to desert,
to forest.
You must learn
to be
where your heart is,
wherever your feet take you,
always
here
in the present.

Prickly Love

Beside the Gila River

ELK DANCE

Wind in my favor
the elk dance before me
unaware,
prancing and huffing,
heads held high,
a clatter of hooves
and antlers,
radiant brown coats flowing
behind evergreens.

MOGOLLON RIM

Elk sign all morning
on the last of red earth
for many miles.
Everett Ruess ascended
this slope,
weaving between manzanita,
oak, and ponderosa,
to find a snowy forest
over the lip
and see the desert
stretching out below.
He must have known
this bed of slickrock,
this magical edge
poised between
worlds.
Perhaps his hand
touched this juniper
as he looked out
across the land,
memorizing the shadows,
holding them close
to his heart.

Oakside

SECRET

Carrying Clear Creek
upslope
through the pines,
water swaying in my pack,
a shiny white treasure
stops me.
Elk antler
dropped
on the trail.
I gather it like a treasure,
hiding it
the same way
I've hidden others,
tucked tight
against the trunk
of an alligator juniper tree,
safe to weather
into dust.

SHADOW

Wind through wing beats
   goshawk rises
      prey in talons
         disappears
            in the forest.

Pusch Ridge Wilderness

Inner Gorge, Colorado River

PREDATOR

It happened before
on the Tonto Trail,
Bighorn sheep rushing
in front of me,
two arm lengths away —
but this time
a hundred elk
racing, bisect the trail,
chased by something
far more threatening
than me.
And in the wake
of their passing,
that potent silence,
those prickly sensations.
I walk faster,
eyes darting
to the empty space
from whence they emerged,
searching for the cause
of commotion.

OUTSIDE FLAGSTAFF

Two signs:
"Mexico 610 Miles" and "Utah 190 Miles."
My God,
what an awful
long way
to walk.

First View, San Francisco Peaks

New Snow, Aspens

ASPENS

Morning light
on quakies
submerged
in winter snow.
Is anything
more glorious?
And yet they end
mysteriously
on a slope
scattered near
the edge of ponderosas,
white trunks
disappearing
behind me
as I walk north,
entering oceans
of pinyon and juniper.

FEATHERS

Mid-day rest
sheltered by junipers
and somehow I know
that Tom is dead,
his memory so close
it floods out every pore,
forcing me to my knees,
sobbing.

When I rise
I find four
tiny blue feathers,
one for each direction.
I carry them
all the way to Utah.
I carry them
still.

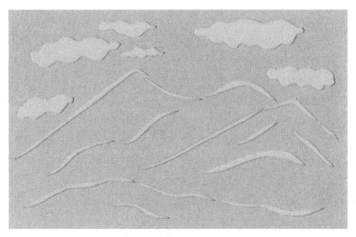

Lava Peaks

GRAND CANYON

Lava desert rolls
in hills of pinyon and juniper
stretching forever
to each horizon.
Nothing south of the rim
indicates
the chasm exists,
beyond mere glimpses
of Kaibab limestone,
far away, covered in trees.
There is no warning
until the trees part
and your feet pause at the edge
of that stunning gorge.

And oh how the early ones,
not knowing,
must have felt
their hearts sink
to their toes
upon seeing this obstacle,
this impenetrable canyon,
so disappointing
to white explorers
who declared the region valueless.
But here I am,
155 years after Colonel Joseph C. Ives
said no one would ever visit.
Burnt cinnamon-vanilla scented
ponderosa trees share the view
and no matter how many times
I stand at the rim,
each time
is new.

WORDS

All the words
of past or present
lovers,
positive or negative,
we carry them
with us.
All the words of our mothers
and fathers,
teachers, friends, siblings, rivals,
even strangers,
we carry them
in our hearts
everywhere
we walk.
May all our words
coming in
or going out
be soft,
be kind.

May all our words
dwell peacefully
in every heart.
May our words
be gentle,
mindful,
reflecting
good intentions,
and easy
to carry.

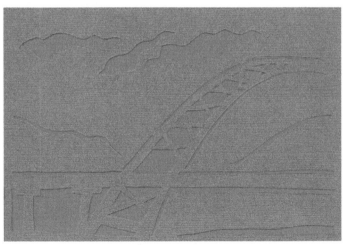

Roosevelt Bridge

REDWALL LIMESTONE

The world
hums
with
vermilion light.

Vermilion Delights

ORACLE RIDGE

In all this time
I wasn't ever alone.
There was wind
and rock,
applause
from lanes of purple lupine,
Red-tailed hawks
and metallic beetles,
life
delighting
in every second.
Solo, yes
of course,
but never alone,
not me.

GENESIS

Follow your dreams
and the path
will be covered
in flowers
and light,
ending as it should
with wind,
and rain,
a spark of lightning,
the smell
of wet earth,
thunder on the horizon,
and friends
to welcome you home.